CONTENTS

KT-394-224

THE FIFA WORLD CUP

The FIFA World Cup is a football tournament that takes place every four years. Thirty-two teams from around the world compete at this tournament. The first World Cup took place in Uruguay in 1930, and the host nation won after an exciting final match against Argentina.

In 2014 Brazil will host the 20th edition of the World Cup. The tournament is extremely popular with football fans all over the world, and every four years excitement and anticipation builds towards the next tournament. The fans hope to see their favourite players performing at the highest level and expect to witness great moments of skill and effort.

OUTSTANDING PERFORMANCES

At every World Cup there have been outstanding teams, surprising results, lots of goals, and above all, great players. These star footballers have amazed crowds and television audiences all over the world with their incredible displays of skill.

This book is full of great footballers who have performed brilliantly at the World Cup. These players may have scored or saved lots of goals. Some were great captains, who guided their teammates all the way to the final.

Whatever their talents, these players have done something special at the World Cup, and they deserve their place among the World Cup heroes.

Find out which player has appeared in the most World Cup finals on page 36.

Find out who is the World Cup record goalscorer on page 18.

Find out which player scored Japan's first ever World Cup goal on page 26.

WORLD CUP FEVER

WORLD CUP HEROES

Michael Hurley

Raintree is an imprint of Capstone Global Library
Limited, a company incorporated in England and
Wales having its registered office at 7 Pilgrim
Street, London, EC4V 6LB – Registered company
number: 6695582

www.raintreepublishers.co.uk
myorders@raintreepublishers.co.uk.

Edited by Claire Throp and Vaarunika Dharmapala
Designed by Joanna Hinton-Malivoire
Picture research by Hannah Taylor
Originated by Capstone Global Library Limited
Printed and bound in China by Leo Paper Products

ISBN 978 1 406 26624 5 (hardback)
17 16 15 14 13
10 9 8 7 6 5 4 3 2 1

ISBN 978 1 406 26629 0 (paperback)
17 16 15 14 13
10 9 8 7 6 5 4 3 2 1

**British Library Cataloguing in Publication
Data**
Hurley, Michael.
World Cup heroes. -- (World Cup fever)
796.3′346640922-dc23
A full catalogue record for this book is available
from the British Library.

Acknowledgements
We would like to thank the following for
permission to reproduce photographs: Corbis pp.
29 (Colorsport/Andrew Cowie); Getty Images
pp. 5 (Javier Soriano/AFP), 10, 22, 23 & 25
(Bob Thomas), 12 & 38 (Popperfoto), 15 (Daniel
Garcia/AFP), 24 (Georges Gobet/AFP), 30 (Henri
Szwarc/Bongarts), 31 (Nicholas Kamm/AFP),
36 (Alex Livesey), 40 (Gabriel Bouys/AFP), 41
(George Tiedemann /Sports Illustrated), 43 (Rich
Schultz); Photoshot pp. 9, 19, 32 & 33 (Kyodo), 11
(Picture Alliance), 20 (Picture Alliance/DPA), 21
(Markus Gilliar/Actionplus); Press Association pp.
7, 16, 17, 26, 27 & 35 (Empics), 34 & 37 AP Photo);
Rex Features p. 39.

All background images courtesy of Shutterstock.

Cover photograph of Pelé celebrating with
Jairzinho after scoring the first goal against Brazil
at the FIFA World Cup final in Mexico, 1970
reproduced with permission of Press Association
(Sven Simon).

URUGUAY 1930: THE FIRST HEROES

The first FIFA World Cup competition had only 13 entrants, including France, USA, Argentina, and Brazil.

Uruguay, the host nation, beat Argentina 4–2 in the final to win the tournament. It was an exciting match, where Uruguay had to come back from 2–1 behind at half-time!

DID YOU KNOW?

Guillermo Stabile was the first winner of the award for World Cup top goalscorer. The top goalscorer is given an award called the "Golden Shoe" for their achievement. The Golden Shoe award is now known as the "Golden Boot", and is still given to the highest goalscorer at each World Cup.

HAT-TRICK MAGIC

Uruguay's top goalscorer at the first World Cup was Pedro Cea. He was an experienced international footballer by the time his country hosted the World Cup. He had played for his country at the 1924 and 1928 Olympics, helping them to win the gold medal at both tournaments. Cea scored a wonderful hat-trick in the World Cup semi-final against Yugoslavia, helping his team to win the match 6–1. In the final, Cea scored the important equalizing goal. His team didn't look back after Cea's goal, scoring another two to win the match.

▼ Uruguay scores their third goal against Argentina at the 1930 World Cup final.

EIGHT WORLD CUP GOALS!

Argentina's outstanding player at the 1930 tournament was Guillermo Stábile. He scored one of Argentina's goals in the 4–2 final defeat. In total, Stábile scored an incredible eight goals in four matches, and he was the 1930 World Cup top goalscorer.

PLAYER

Guillermo Stábile

National team: Argentina
Date of birth: 17/01/1906
World Cup appearances: 4 (1930)

PLAYER

Pedro Cea

National team: Uruguay
Date of birth: 01/09/1900
World Cup appearances: 4 (1930)

GREAT GOALKEEPERS

In the history of the World Cup there have been some outstanding goalkeepers.

Some have used their skills and experience to help their country to win the World Cup. Others have stood out because of their style of goalkeeping or because they made great saves. This chapter is dedicated to World Cup goalkeeping heroes.

CAPTAIN CASILLAS

Spain's goalkeeper and captain Iker Casillas helped to guide his team to victory in the 2010 FIFA World Cup. His experience, composure, and leadership were vital in Spain's journey to the final in South Africa. With their captain Iker Casillas in goal, Spain only conceded two goals in the whole tournament.

Casillas' performance in the 2010 final was outstanding and he made important saves to keep the score at 0–0. Spain eventually broke the deadlock in the 116th minute in extra time and scored what turned out to be the winning goal. The final score was 1–0 to Spain, and Casillas and his team celebrated winning the World Cup for the first time in Spain's history.

THREE AND COUNTING...

Iker Casillas has played for Spain at three World Cups. He played in his first World Cup match in South Korea in 2002, when Spain beat Slovenia 3–1. In total, Casillas has played in 15 World Cup matches, and he has only been on the losing side three times.

PLAYER

Iker Casillas

National team: Spain
Date of birth: 20/5/1981
World Cup appearances:
15 (2002, 2006, 2010)

DID YOU KNOW?

Casillas' excellent performance in goal for Spain during the 2010 World Cup earned him the award for best goalkeeper at the tournament. Here, he raises the trophy in celebration.

WORLD CUP WINNING CAPTAIN

Dino Zoff was the goalkeeper and captain for Italy when they won the FIFA World Cup in 1982. Zoff played well in the group stage, only conceding two goals. He also made a crucial save against Brazil in a very close 3–2 win in the second round.

A GREAT WAY TO FINISH

Winning the 1982 World Cup final was a fitting end to this great goalkeeper's career for Italy. Zoff retired after the final, having played for Italy 111 times and at three World Cups.

PLAYER

Dino Zoff

National team: Italy

Date of birth: 28/02/1942

World Cup appearances: 17 (1974, 1978, 1982)

DID YOU KNOW?

Dino Zoff is the oldest player in World Cup history to win the tournament. He was 40 years old when he received the trophy for Italy.

WORLD CUP SENSATION

Rene Higuita (see above, right) was the Colombia goalkeeper during the 1990 FIFA World Cup in Italy. This was his only World Cup tournament, but when it was over most football fans around the world knew all about Rene Higuita.

A NEW BREED OF GOALKEEPER

Higuita had an unusual style of goalkeeping. He liked to play football on the pitch like the other members of his team, and would often come out of the 18-yard box and dribble with the ball. He seemed to like the danger of

trying to play against the opposition strikers. He did not always get away with it, though! In Colombia's match with Cameroon he lost control of the ball, and Cameroon scored. Despite this mistake, fans loved Higuita's style and he certainly stood out on the pitch with his bright goalkeeping jersey and his big hair.

Gordon Banks

National team: England

Date of birth: 30/12/1937

World Cup appearances: 9
(1966, 1970)

GORDON BANKS, ENGLAND, AND 1966

The 1966 World Cup was played in England – and it was England, with Gordon Banks in goal, that won the tournament. Banks did not allow a shot past him in England's first four matches. The only goal Banks conceded up until the final was a penalty in the 82nd minute of the semi-final versus Portugal.

DID YOU KNOW?

In nine World Cup matches with Banks in goal, England only lost once. The match was against Brazil in 1970. Banks conceded only four goals in total – an incredible record for a goalkeeper at the World Cup.

THE GREATEST SAVE?

At the World Cup in Mexico in 1970, Gordon Banks made an outstanding save that many people think is the greatest ever in a World Cup match. The save was incredible because of Bank's amazing agility, and because it was made against the Brazilian player Pelé, one of the finest footballers ever (see page 38). When Pelé headed the ball towards goal, Banks somehow managed to scramble across the goal line and tip the ball away with his fingers. It was an amazing save.

FIFA GOALKEEPING AWARD

Lev Yashin was a fantastic goalkeeper and he played for the Soviet Union at three World Cups. He was particularly good at stopping goal-bound strikes because he was tall and very agile. Yashin was so good in goal that FIFA named an award in his honour. Until 2010 the award given to the goalkeeper who has performed best at each World Cup was called the "Lev Yashin Award". It is now known as the "Golden Glove".

PLAYER

Lev Yashin

National team: Soviet Union
Date of birth: 22/10/1929
World Cup appearances: 13
(1958, 1962, 1966)

ONE-HIT WONDERS

This chapter is dedicated to the footballers who had only one opportunity to perform at the FIFA World Cup.

This collection of World Cup stars were able to perform to the highest standard on the biggest stage in football and in front of one of the largest audiences of sports fans in the world. All of these players took their chance to show the world that they could be World Cup heroes!

BECOMING A LEGEND

Not many football fans around the world knew who Salvatore Schillaci was before the 1990 World Cup.

By the time the tournament finished, all that had changed! Schillaci appeared in all of Italy's matches in 1990, and he scored in all but one of them. Schillaci finished the tournament with six goals.

LOSING AT HOME

The pressure for Italy to get to the final was intense as they were playing in their own country. Schillaci did his best for his team by scoring again in the semi-final against Argentina. It was his fifth goal. The match ended 1–1 after extra time, and Italy lost on penalties. Schillaci ended the tournament the way he started it by scoring again in the play-off match against England.

PLAYER

Salvatore Schillaci

National team: Italy

Date of birth: 01/12/1964

World Cup appearances: 7 (1990)

DID YOU KNOW?

Before the 1990 World Cup, Schillaci had not scored for Italy and he had only played for his country once. Schillaci finished the tournament as the highest scorer, and he walked away with the FIFA Golden Boot award.

Johan Cruyff

National team: The Netherlands

Date of birth: 25/04/1947

World Cup appearances: 7 (1974)

OUTSTANDING PLAYER

Johan Cruyff (see above, left) was one of the greatest ever footballers. He had amazing ball control and he was able to dribble the ball and pass it precisely. He could also shoot very accurately. Cruyff's only World Cup tournament was in 1974, when he was the outstanding player in a very talented Dutch team. The Netherlands reached the final and they were unfortunate to lose 2–1 against West Germany.

WORLD CUP GOALS

Cruyff scored three goals in seven matches in 1974. They were very important goals for his team. He scored twice against Argentina and once against Brazil. This was a special goal. Cruyff used his tremendous technique to control a volleyed shot past the Brazil goalkeeper.

FOUR-GOAL HERO

Eusébio (see below, left) was the star of the Portugal team at the 1966 World Cup. His extraordinary performances for Portugal helped the team to reach the semi-finals for the first time in their history. Eusébio scored nine goals in six matches – a terrific record. His nine goals included a stunning four goals against North Korea in a dramatic 5–3 win when Portugal struck back after being 3–0 behind. Eusébio's power and pace worried the North Korean defenders again and again, and his powerful strikes were too hot for the goalkeeper to handle.

ON THE SPOT

Portugal lost 2–1 in the semi-final to the eventual World Cup winners, England. Eusébio scored a penalty near the end of the match. He then scored another penalty in the third-place play-off match, as Portugal beat the Soviet Union 2–1.

PLAYER

Eusébio

National Team: Portugal
Date of birth: 25/01/1942
World Cup appearances: 6 (1966)

GREAT GOALSCORERS

Footballers who can score goals are vital to their team.

Teams with one or more players with the ability to score great goals usually do well at the World Cup. Here is a selection of some of the greatest goal-scoring World Cup heroes.

WORLD CUP GREATEST GOALSCORER

Brazilian striker Ronaldo has scored more goals at the World Cup than any other player in history. This is a fantastic achievement. He was also the winner of the Golden Boot award for his performances at the 2002 World Cup.

Ronaldo helped his team to reach the final of the 1998 World Cup. He scored four goals in six matches leading up to the final. However, Ronaldo and his teammates did not play very well in the final against France and lost 3–0.

2002 WORLD CUP HERO

Ronaldo and Brazil went one stage further at the 2002 World Cup – they won it! Ronaldo scored some fantastic goals during Brazil's journey to the final. He scored the crucial goal in a 1–0 win against Turkey, in the semi-final. He followed that by scoring both goals in the World Cup final when Brazil beat Germany 2–0. Ronaldo finished the tournament with a fantastic record of eight goals in seven matches. He was a vital part of Brazil's team, and their opponents could not cope with his pace, power, and shooting skill.

GOALSCORING RECORDS

Top goalscorers in World Cup history:

Ronaldo (Brazil)	15
Gerd Müller (West Germany)	14
Miroslav Klose (Germany)	14
Just Fontaine (France)	13
Pelé (Brazil)	12

Ronaldo

National team: Brazil

Date of birth: 22/09/1976

World Cup appearances: 19
(1994, 1998, 2002, 2006)

PLAYER

PLAYER

Gerd Müller

National team: West Germany

Date of birth: 03/11/1945

World Cup appearances: 13
(1970, 1974)

DID YOU KNOW?

West Germany reached the final of the World Cup in 1974 and during the tournament Müller scored another four goals to add to his 1970 tally. Müller ended up with an incredible record of 14 goals in 13 World Cup matches.

1970 GOLDEN BOOT WINNER

Gerd Müller was a great player who helped his team to reach the World Cup final in 1974 and scored the winning goal. The West Germany striker scored an incredible ten goals at the 1970 tournament, and won the Golden Boot award. His team were unfortunate to miss out on the final in 1970, losing a very close semi-final 4–3 against Italy.

ANOTHER MÜLLER!

Another German named Müller won the award for top scorer at the 2010 World Cup. Thomas Müller was a very important member of a vibrant, young German team that reached the semi-finals. His five goals, plus three assists, earned him the Golden Boot. He was also awarded the FIFA Best Young Player Award.

PLAYER

Thomas Müller

National team: Germany

Date of birth: 13/09/1989

World Cup appearances: 6 (2010)

20

TOP GOALSCORER

Just *incroyable*! Fontaine's 1958 World Cup goals:

3 vs Paraguay (7–3)
2 vs Yugoslavia (2–3)
1 vs Scotland (2–1)
2 vs N. Ireland (4–0)
1 vs Brazil (2–5)
4 vs W. Germany (6–3)

TOP GOALSCORER

France striker Just Fontaine was a goalscoring hero for his country. Fontaine scored an incredible 13 goals in six matches at the World Cup in 1958, in Sweden. This remains the record for the most goals scored at one tournament.

ITALY'S HERO

Paolo Rossi became Italy's hero at the World Cup in 1982 after a fantastic performance in their match against Brazil. Italy won a dramatic match 3–2, and Rossi scored a hat-trick. He continued his excellent form in Italy's next match against Poland, scoring both goals in a 2–0 win. Italy beat West Germany 3–1 in the World Cup final, and Rossi scored the first goal of the match.

Paolo Rossi ended up with the Golden Boot award for top goalscorer with six goals, and he was given the FIFA Golden Ball award for best player at the tournament.

PLAYER

Paolo Rossi

National team: Italy

Date of birth: 23/09/1956

World Cup appearances: 14 (1978, 1982)

DID YOU KNOW?

Italy striker Paolo Rossi scored in his first-ever World Cup match in 1978. In 1982 he scored in his last match, the World Cup final.

1986 GOLDEN BOOT WINNER

Gary Lineker was England's goal-scoring hero at the 1986 World Cup. He scored six goals, including a first-half hat-trick in England's 3–0 win against Poland. Lineker won the 1986 Golden Boot award.

PENALTIES AND SEMI-FINAL DEFEAT

In 1990 England made it all the way to the semi-final. Lineker scored two penalties to help his team to a 3–2 win in the quarter-final against Cameroon. In the semi-final against West Germany he scored a very good goal in the 80th minute to level the score at 1–1. After extra time, England lost the match 4–3 on penalties.

DID YOU KNOW?

Gary Lineker scored a total of ten goals in 12 World Cup matches.

Gary Lineker

National team: England

Date of birth: 30/11/1960

World Cup appearances: 12 (1986, 1990)

WORLD OF HEROES

This chapter is dedicated to players from many different countries who have left their mark on the World Cup.

WONDERFUL GOAL

Dennis Bergkamp was an important player for the Netherlands at two World Cups and scored one of the greatest goals ever seen. In the 1998 quarter-final, Bergkamp's last-minute goal guaranteed his team a place in the semi-final. The goal was amazing. Bergkamp used his excellent ball skills to control a long pass, touch the ball past a defender, and then volley his shot past the goalkeeper. The ball flew into the top corner of the goal.

PLAYER

Dennis Bergkamp

National team: The Netherlands
Date of birth: 10/05/1969
World Cup appearances: 12 (1994, 1998)

WORLD CUP SENSATION

Saeed Al-Owairan was not very well known to football fans before the 1994 World Cup. After his performance in Saudi Arabia's last group match versus Belgium, he became an overnight star.

"GOAL OF THE TOURNAMENT"

In the fifth minute, Al-Owairan received a pass from a teammate in his own half of the pitch and started to run with the ball.

He crossed the halfway line and took the ball easily past two Belgian players. He continued to dribble the ball, and went past another opposition player. As he entered the 18-yard box he was faced with two defenders and the goalkeeper. He managed to keep his cool and shoot the ball into the top corner of the goal. Al-Owairan's run and goal happened so fast it was like a blur! One commentator for the match said it was the "greatest goal of the tournament".

AUSTRALIA'S HERO

Australian midfielder Tim Cahill became his country's hero in 2006 when he scored the first goal by an Australian in the history of the World Cup. In 2010 Australia qualified for their second consecutive World Cup, and Tim Cahill had an up-and-down tournament. He was sent off in the match against Germany, but returned to the team for the last group match against Serbia. Cahill scored a goal, and was named Man of the Match for his performance. Australia won the match 2–1, but unfortunately for Cahill and his team they were knocked out of the competition.

PLAYER

Tim Cahill

National team: Australia

Date of birth: 06/12/1979

World Cup appearances: 6 (2006, 2010)

JAPAN'S HERO

Japan's first ever World Cup appearance did not go very well. After qualifying for the 1998 tournament in France, their incredibly enthusiastic fans had high hopes for the team. Unfortunately Japan lost all three group matches. The highlight of the 1998 World Cup for Japan was the performance of Mashashi Nakayama. He was Japan's hero after he scored their first ever goal at the World Cup.

PLAYER

Mashashi Nakayama

National team: Japan

Date of birth: 23/09/1967

World Cup appearances: 4 (1998)

IRELAND'S GOALSCORING HERO

The Republic of Ireland had played four matches at the World
Cup before they won their first match in regulation time.
Ray Houghton (see below, centre) was the hero for Ireland
when they beat Italy 1–0 at the 1994 World Cup in the United
States. Houghton's goal came from a volleyed shot from
outside the 18-yard box. His goal celebration was fantastic
and his goal secured Houghton's place in the hearts of Irish
fans forever.

PLAYER

Ray Houghton

National team: Republic of Ireland

Date of birth: 09/01/1962

World Cup appearances: 9
(1990, 1994, 1998)

THE BRAZILIANS

Players do not have to score the winning goal or be on the winning team in the final to become a hero at the World Cup. In the two World Cup tournaments held in the 1980s, the Brazil team became heroes to football fans all over the world. This was due to their amazing skill and the way they excited the crowds who watched them play.

PLAYER

Zico

National team: Brazil
Date of birth: 03/03/1953
World Cup appearances: 14

PLAYER

Falcao

National team: Brazil
Date of birth: 16/10/1953
World Cup appearances: 7

GREAT GOALSCORERS

In 1982 Zico and Falcao shared seven goals as Brazil tore their opponents apart in the early matches of the competition. Brazil scored four goals in two consecutive matches against Scotland and New Zealand, and another three goals in a 3–1 victory against Argentina. They then narrowly missed out on getting to the World Cup semi-final when they were beaten 3–2 by Italy.

Brazil continued their dynamic, attacking football at the 1986 World Cup in Mexico. They were unlucky to lose in a penalty shoot-out against France in the quarter-final. Brazil striker Careca ended the tournament with five goals and was the runner-up for the Golden Boot award.

PLAYER

Careca

National team: Brazil
Date of birth: 05/10/1960
World Cup appearances: 9

BRAZIL'S LEADER

A group of players with amazing skill, power, pace, and shooting ability needs a leader on the pitch. Brazil had this player in the 1980s. His name was Socrates (see below, second from the right), and his calmness, brilliant passing ability, and eye for goal helped Brazil win new fans all over the world.

PLAYER

Socrates

National team: Brazil
Date of birth: 19/02/1954
World Cup appearances: 10

1990 GOAL-SCORING HERO

Roger Milla was one of the first African World Cup heroes when he helped his Cameroon team to the quarter-final of the 1990 tournament. This was the first time an African nation had gone so far in the competition. Eight years after their World Cup debut in 1982, Cameroon qualified for the tournament in Italy. Cameroon started magnificently, winning 1–0 against Argentina in the opening match. In their next match against Romania, Milla was the goal-scoring hero. His two goals ensured a 2–1 victory for Cameroon and a place in the next round.

PLAYER

Roger Milla

National team: Cameroon

Date of birth: 20/05/1952

World Cup appearances: 10 (1982, 1990, 1994)

Milla continued his goal-scoring form in Cameroon's match against Colombia. He made the score 1–0 with a powerful shot and then followed that with another goal two minutes later.

BEST YOUNG PLAYER

Landon Donovan is the all-time leading goalscorer in United States history. He is also his country's leading goalscorer at the World Cup. At the 2002 World Cup, Donovan was presented with the FIFA Best Young Player Award. He was rewarded for his exciting displays, and for scoring important goals. He had helped his country to their best-ever finish at the World Cup, reaching the quarter-final.

NATIONAL HERO

After a very disappointing 2006 World Cup, Donovan and his United States teammates played much better in 2010 in South Africa. Donovan scored three goals, including a vital one against Algeria, to win the match 1–0. His performances at the World Cup have made Landon Donovan a national hero.

PLAYER

Landon Donovan

National team: United States

Date of birth: 04/03/1982

World Cup appearances: 12
(2002, 2006, 2010)

2010 WORLD CUP HEROES

There were some great moments during the 2010 FIFA World Cup.

These included performances from Ghana's Sulley Muntari, Japan's Keisuke Honda, the Netherlands' Giovanni van Bronkhorst, and Argentina's Carlos Tevez. They all scored amazing goals from long distances.

MULTIPLE AWARDS

A football star who really shone during the 2010 World Cup was Diego Forlan. The Uruguay striker was playing in his second World Cup after appearing in 2002. He only started one match in 2002, and scored one goal. In 2010 Forlan finished the tournament as the joint highest goalscorer. He was also given the award for best goal, and the Golden Ball for best player at the World Cup.

Forlan scored five goals, including two shots from distance, one free kick, a volley, and a penalty. He showed excellent technique throughout the competition and led his team by example. He was courageous and determined, and guided Uruguay to fourth place – their best finish at the World Cup since 1970.

PLAYER

Diego Forlan

National team: Uruguay
Date of birth: 19/05/1979
World Cup appearances: 8 (2002, 2010)

Andrés Iniesta

National team: Spain
Date of birth: 11/05/1984
World Cup appearances: 7 (2010)

VERY IMPORTANT PLAYER

Another outstanding player at the 2010 World Cup was Spain's Andrés Iniesta (see above, holding trophy). He scored the goal that made Spain World Cup champions for the first time. His status as a hero was confirmed when he calmly shot the ball past the Holland goalkeeper in the 116th minute of the final.

Iniesta played in all but one of Spain's matches at the 2010 World Cup, and he was one of their most important players. He is a fantastic footballer who can pass and shoot accurately, and he appears to stay calm at all times.

COURAGEOUS CAPTAINS

Being chosen to captain your country at the World Cup is an honour for any footballer.

Captains are usually experienced players who are respected by the other members of the squad. Helping to guide their team to glory – and lifting the World Cup trophy – is a moment that will be treasured forever by the players and football fans all over the world.

PLAYER AND MANAGER

Franz Beckenbauer was the first person to win the World Cup both as a player and also as a manager. He was the captain in 1974 and the manager in 1990 when West Germany won the tournament.

PLAYER

Franz Beckenbauer

National team: West Germany

Date of birth: 11/09/1945

World Cup appearances: 18 (1966, 1970, 1974)

Italy's Fabio Cannavaro was a highly respected defender who played for his country a record 136 times and appeared at four World Cup tournaments. Cannavaro captained the Italy team when they won the World Cup in 2006 in Germany. The Italy defenders put on an amazing performance as the team made their way to the final.

Cannavaro's presence in the centre of Italy's defence saw them concede only one goal in the six matches leading up to the final. This was an incredible achievement. In the final, Italy beat France on penalties to win the World Cup trophy after the match had ended in a 1–1 draw after extra time.

DID YOU KNOW?

Fabio Cannavaro was rewarded for leading Italy to glory in the 2006 World Cup when he won the award for 2006 FIFA World Player of the Year. He became the first defender ever to win the award.

PLAYER

Fabio Cannavaro

National team: Italy

Date of birth: 13/09/1973

World Cup appearances: 18 (2006, 2010)

CAFU

Marcos Evangelista de Moraes is better known to millions of football fans as "Cafu". Cafu was the Brazil right-back who played at four World Cups, and he was the captain when Brazil won the tournament for a record fifth time in 2002. Cafu was a substitute in three matches during the 1994 tournament, including the final, which Brazil won against Italy. In 1998 Cafu played in all but one of Brazil's matches, including the final.

LEADING HIS TEAM TO GLORY

Cafu started the 2002 World Cup as Brazil's captain, and helped to lead his team all the way to the final and World Cup success. Brazil won the final 2–0 against Germany. Cafu lifted the World Cup trophy and celebrated winning the tournament for the second time in his career.

PLAYER

Cafu

National team: Brazil

Date of birth: 07/06/1970

World Cup appearances: 20 (1994, 1998, 2002, 2006)

DID YOU KNOW?

In 2002 Cafu became the first player to appear in three World Cup finals. In total, Cafu played in 20 World Cup matches and was on the winning side 16 times!

ENGLAND'S WORLD CUP CAPTAIN

Bobby Moore played for England 108 times in his career, including 90 appearances as captain. Moore played in every match for England at the 1962, 1966, and 1970 World Cup tournaments.

Moore was the captain of the England team that won the 1966 World Cup on home soil. England beat West Germany in a tightly contested World Cup final. When Moore, as captain, received the Jules Rimet trophy from the Queen, he instantly became a hero to all England football fans.

PLAYER

Bobby Moore

National team: England

Date of birth: 12/04/1941

World Cup appearances: 14 (1962, 1966, 1970)

THE GREATEST
WORLD CUP STARS

This chapter looks at three World Cup winners who became heroes because of their amazing ability, skill, and determination.

These outstanding footballers are considered by many football fans to be the greatest World Cup heroes of all time.

PLAYER

Pelé

National team: Brazil

Date of birth: 23/10/1940

World Cup appearances: 14 (1958, 1962, 1966, 1970)

PELÉ: THE LEGEND

Possibly the greatest footballer ever, and two-time World Cup winner, Pelé played for Brazil at four World Cup tournaments, scoring goals in the 1958 and 1970 finals.

Pelé made his World Cup debut at just 17 years old, when he produced some amazing performances at the 1958 World Cup. His play in the final was mesmerizing and the Sweden defenders could not stop him. He scored two goals – and one in particular showed off his tremendous skills. After receiving a pass on the chest, he instantly managed to control the ball, take it past one defender, and deftly volley it into the back of the net.

THE GREATEST TEAM EVER?

The Brazil team that won the 1970 tournament is considered by many football fans to be the greatest ever. Pelé and his teammates tore the opposition apart and scored at least three goals in five out of six matches, including the final. Pelé's four goals at the 1970 World Cup included the opening goal in the final when Brazil convincingly beat Italy 4–1.

GOAL-SCORING HERO

Pelé had many of the attributes that make up a great footballer. He could pass, tackle, and head the ball as well, if not better, than anyone else. But his greatest weapon at World Cup tournaments was his ability to score goals. In a total of 14 World Cup matches, Pelé scored an incredible 12 goals.

FRANCE'S STAR PLAYER

France won their first and only World Cup tournament on home soil in 1998. The star player of the French team was Zinedine Zidane who scored twice in the final to give France a convincing 3–0 win against Brazil.

PLAYER

Zinedine Zidane

National team: France

Date of birth: 23/06/1972

World Cup appearances: 12 (1998, 2002, 2006)

RED CARD AND GOLDEN BALL

Zidane ended his international football career at the 2006 World Cup. However, it was not the perfect ending that many football fans were hoping for.

In the 110th minute in extra time in the final, Zidane was sent off by the referee for head-butting an opponent in the chest. Despite his misdemeanour in the final, Zidane's amazing performances during the 2006 tournament won him the prestigious FIFA Golden Ball award.

CENTRE OF ATTENTION

Diego Maradona played for Argentina at four World Cups and he was always at the centre of attention – and controversy. Maradona had amazing skill and ball control, and his dribbling ability was sensational. With Maradona in their team, Argentina fans knew that anything was possible. His performances at the 1986 tournament were stunning and he showed off his amazing dribbling skills and scored some great goals. Maradona led his team all the way to victory in the final against West Germany. In 1990 Maradona once again led his team to the final. However, this time they lost 1–0 to West Germany.

CONTROVERSIAL FIGURE

Although Maradona is a World Cup hero to many football fans, his career will always be tainted by controversy. He scored a goal with his hand at the 1986 World Cup match against England and was suspended for illegal drug use at the 1994 World Cup. Despite his flaws, Maradona will always be remembered for his positive impact on the World Cup tournament.

PLAYER

Diego Maradona

National team: Argentina
Date of birth: 30/10/1960
World Cup appearances: 21
(1982, 1986, 1990, 1994)

WHO WILL BE A HERO IN 2014?

The 2014 FIFA World Cup will be packed with exciting footballers. Here are a few well-known players who have the potential to produce extraordinary performances.

OUTSTANDING PLAYER

Lionel Messi (see opposite, centre) has won many trophies as a player with the Barcelona team. His achievements for Barcelona have seen him receive many awards for his outstanding skill and ability. Messi made his World Cup debut in 2006, when he came on in the 75th minute of Argentina's opening match against Serbia and scored his first World Cup goal. There was a lot of pressure and expectation for Messi and Argentina in 2010. Messi performed well, but not to his best standard, and was unable to score in any of his team's matches.

PLAYER

Lionel Messi

National team: Argentina
Date of birth: 24/06/1987
World Cup appearances: 8 (2006, 2010)

THE NEXT GENERATION

When Brazil hosts the World Cup in 2014, their star player could be Neymar (see opposite, left). The exciting young striker scored 17 goals in his first 27 appearances for his country. This is a fantastic start to his international career. Neymar will be only 22 years old when he plays at his first World Cup, but there will be a lot of pressure on him and his team to succeed. Although he is young, Neymar is expected to attract a lot of attention in the 2014 tournament because of his dynamic skills, his dribbling ability, and his powerful shots.

PLAYER

Neymar

National team: Brazil
Date of birth: 05/02/1992
World Cup appearances: 0

WORLD CUP 2014...

Cristiano Ronaldo will play in his third World Cup in 2014. He is Portugal's captain, and their most creative player. Ronaldo has won most of the trophies on offer to a footballer at club level. The only trophy missing in his fantastic career is the World Cup. Could 2014 be Ronaldo's and Portugal's year to triumph?

PLAYER

Cristiano Ronaldo

National team: Portugal

Date of birth: 05/02/1985

World Cup appearances: 10 (2006, 2010)

GLOSSARY

18-yard box area around the goal, also known as the penalty area

agile able to move quickly and easily

assist the last pass that leads to a goal being scored

composure being calm and staying in control of yourself

concede allow. For example, if a goalkeeper concedes a goal, he allows it to pass into the net.

consecutive in a row

crucial extremely important

debut someone making their first appearance. For example, a footballer playing at the World Cup for the first time is making their debut.

dribble kicking the ball in front of you as you run forward

equalizing goal that levels the score of the match

extra time extra period of play that is added to a football match if it is a draw at the end of regulation time (90 minutes). Extra time lasts for 30 minutes, with two halves of 15 minutes each.

Fédération Internationale de Football Association (FIFA) international organization responsible for football around the world

FIFA Best Young Player award award given to the young player who has performed best at the World Cup

free kick kick of the ball awarded by the referee after a foul

hat-trick when a player scores three goals in one match it is called a "hat-trick"

Jules Rimet trophy original World Cup trophy named in honour of former FIFA president Jules Rimet

Man of the Match award given to the outstanding player in any football match

mesmerizing taking all of a person's attention

misdemeanour moment of bad behaviour

Olympics international athletic competition held every four years

prestigious something that is very important or special

send off when a referee shows a red card to a player, either for a serious foul or for two yellow cards, the player has to leave the field of play

Soviet Union former union of Eastern European countries, including Russia, which broke up in 1991

substitute player who replaces another player during a match

technique particular way of doing something

valuable very useful or important

vibrant bright, or full of energy

volley act of kicking the ball before it touches the ground

West Germany between 1945 and 1990 Germany was split into two countries: West Germany and East Germany

Yugoslavia former nation in Eastern Europe made up of several modern-day countries, including Serbia and Montenegro

FIND OUT MORE

BOOKS

A–Z of the World Cup (World Cup Fever), Michael Hurley (Raintree, 2014)

Defender (Football Files), Michael Hurley (Raintree, 2011)

Fantastic Football, Clive Gifford (Oxford University Press, 2010)

Goalkeeper (Football Files), Michael Hurley (Raintree, 2011)

Midfielder (Football Files), Michael Hurley (Raintree, 2011)

Soccer (DK: Eyewitness Books), Hugh Hornby (DK Publishing, 2010)

Steven Gerrard (World Cup Heroes), Adam Cottier (John Blake Publishing, 2010

Striker (Football Files), Michael Hurley (Raintree, 2011)

The Kingfisher Football Encyclopaedia, Clive Gifford (Kingfisher, 2010)

Wayne Rooney (World Cup Heroes), Adam Cottier (John Blake Publishing, 2010

World Cup 2014 (World Cup Fever), Michael Hurley (Raintree, 2014)

World Cup Nations (World Cup Fever), Michael Hurley (Raintree, 2014)

WEBSITES

www.fifa.com
The official website for everything World Cup related. You can find the latest team and player news, fixtures, results, and photos.

www.fifa.com/classicfootball/index.html?intcmp=fifacom_hp_module_classic_football
Check out match reports on important World Cup matches from the past, and find out more about some of the greatest ever footballers, football clubs, and stadiums around the world.

www.fifa.com/worldcup/archive/index.html
This is a great place to start if you want to find out facts and stats from previous World Cups.

www.fifa.com/classicfootball/index.html?intcmp=fifacom_hp_module_classic_football

Check out match reports on important World Cup matches from the past, and find out more about some of the greatest ever footballers, football clubs, and stadiums.

www.footballworldcupbrazil2014.com

This unofficial guide to the 2014 World Cup provides videos, blogs, team profiles, and facts and figures about previous World Cup tournaments.

kids.nationalgeographic.co.uk/kids/places/find/brazil

If you want to know more about Brazil, the host of the 2014 World Cup, and the history, geography, and culture of the country, this is a great place to start.

www.goal.com/en-gb/news/3841/world-cup-2014

Check out this website for the latest news on the teams battling to qualify for the World Cup.

LOOK IT UP...

1. There have been many great goalscorers in the World Cup. Do you know or can you find out who scored the fastest goal in World Cup history?

2. Only one player has ever scored a hat-trick in a World Cup final. Do you know who he is and which team he played for?

3. There are so many World Cup players who are considered to be heroes by football fans. Check out a few more of them and find out why they are so admired:

Roberto Baggio (Italy)	Lilian Thuram (France)
Teófilo Cubillas (Peru)	Andreas Brehme (Germany)
Archie Gemmill (Scotland)	Michael Owen (England)

INDEX